Let Freedom Ring

The Boston
Tea Party

by Nancy Furstinger

Consultant:
Nancy M. Godleski
Yale University
New Haven, Connecticut

Bridgestone Books
an imprint of Capstone Press
Mankato, Minnesota

To my nephews, Douglas and Joseph Furstinger and Gregory Nist—boys with adventurous spirits!

Bridgestone Books are published by Capstone Press
151 Good Counsel Drive •P.O. Box 669 • Mankato, Minnesota 56002
http://www.capstone-press.com

Printed in the United States of America

Library of Congress Cataloging-in-Publication Data
Furstinger, Nancy.
      The Boston Tea Party / by Nancy Furstinger.
             p. cm. — (Let freedom ring)
      Includes bibliographical references and index.
      ISBN 0-7368-1093-5
      1. Boston Tea Party, 1773—Juvenile literature. [1. Boston Tea Party, 1773. 2. United States—History—Revolution, 1775–1783—Causes.] I. Title. II. Series.
      E215.7 .F87 2002
      973.3′15—dc21   2001003065

      Summary: Describes the events that led American Patriots to dump British tea into Boston Harbor, an act that precipitated the American Revolution.

Editorial Credits
Rebecca Aldridge, editor; Kia Bielke, cover designer, interior layout designer, and interior illustrator; Jennifer Schonborn, cover production designer; Deirdre Barton, photo researcher

Photo Credits
Cover: North Wind Picture Archives; North Wind Picture Archives, 5, 12, 13, 24, 25, 29, 30, 37, 39 (small); Hulton/Archive Photos, 9; CORBIS, 11, 19, 43; Stock Montage, Inc., 15, 17, 32; Archive Photos, 21; Capstone Press/Gary Sundermeyer, 23; Boston Tea Party Ship & Museum, 27; Index Stock Imagery/Susan Wilson, 35; Archivo Iconografico, S.A./CORBIS, 39 (large); Giraudon/Art Resource, NY, 41

1   2   3   4   5   6   07   06   05   04   03   02

Table of Contents

Chapter One

Trouble Begins to Brew

In the mid-1770s, 2.5 million people lived in the American colonies. The people in one colony were often total strangers to people of the other colonies. The 13 American colonies hugged about 1,500 miles (2,400 kilometers) of the Atlantic coastline. New Hampshire was the northernmost colony, while Georgia was the southernmost colony. Muddy, hole-filled paths were all that linked the colonies together.

In the beginning, the colonies depended on Britain for support. When the first settlers landed their wooden ships at Jamestown, Virginia, in 1607, they welcomed British protection. The long-distance relationship between Britain and its American colonies worked for about 150 years after the settling of Jamestown.

Most colonists never dreamed that the American colonies could unite into a new nation. This belief suited

In the late 1700s, taking a stagecoach was one of the few ways to travel from one American colony to another. The journey included being jolted at top speeds of 8 miles (12.8 kilometers) per hour.

Parliament, Britain's lawmaking body. Britain, the "mother country," treated the colonies like 13 children who should obey without question.

The French and Indian War

Britain and France had fought against one another for hundreds of years. In North America, the two countries fought each other again in the French and Indian War (1754–1763). Britain won the war, and afterward, the American colonies became more independent. They formed their own troops to defend home territory. They formed assemblies, or governments, to make their own laws. Some colonists profited from the war by providing British troops with food and supplies.

At the same time, British debt soared into the millions of dollars. Britain's King George III and Parliament thought it was fair that the colonies help to pay the debt. The king and Parliament reasoned that Britain had protected the colonies from American Indians and the French during the war. The solution seemed clear. Britain should raise money by taxing the colonists.

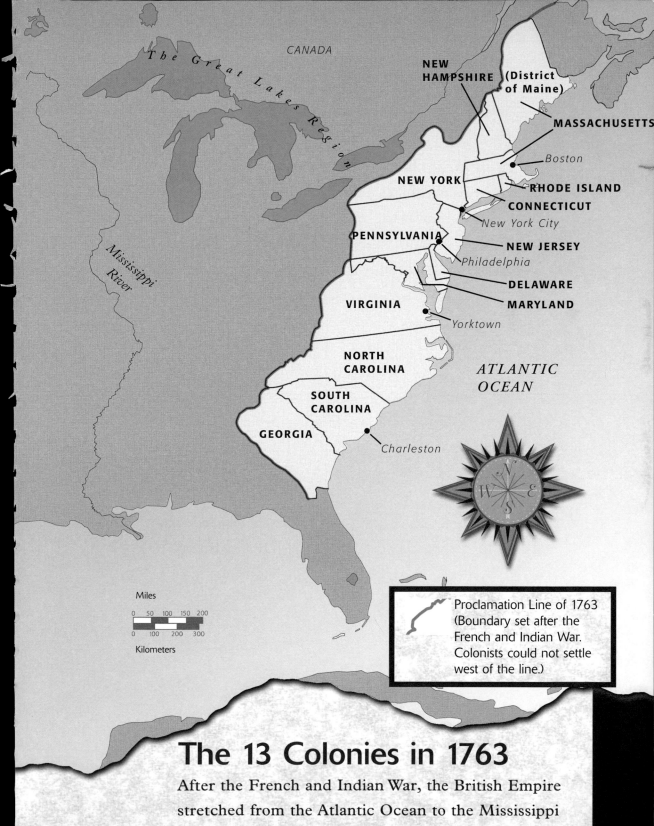

CANADA

The Great Lakes Region

Mississippi River

NEW HAMPSHIRE **(District of Maine)**

MASSACHUSETTS

Boston

NEW YORK

RHODE ISLAND

CONNECTICUT

New York City

PENNSYLVANIA

NEW JERSEY

Philadelphia

DELAWARE

MARYLAND

VIRGINIA

Yorktown

NORTH CAROLINA

ATLANTIC OCEAN

SOUTH CAROLINA

GEORGIA

Charleston

Miles
0 50 100 150 200
0 100 200 300
Kilometers

Proclamation Line of 1763 (Boundary set after the French and Indian War. Colonists could not settle west of the line.)

The 13 Colonies in 1763

After the French and Indian War, the British Empire stretched from the Atlantic Ocean to the Mississippi River and included a large part of Canada.

Thomas Hutchinson

Born in Boston, Thomas Hutchinson (1711–1780) became royal governor of Massachusetts in 1771. As royal governor, he tried to enforce the unpopular Stamp Act. Patriots were upset with his efforts to make sure this law was obeyed. An angry mob destroyed his house in revenge. Hutchinson described the attack:

"Besides my plate [silver items] and family pictures, household furniture of every kind, my own children and servants [clothing, the mob] carried off . . . money and emptied the house of everything whatsoever . . . not leaving a single book or paper in it and have scattered or destroyed all the manuscripts and other papers I had been collecting for 30 years together besides a great number of public papers in my custody [care]."

After the Boston Tea Party, Hutchinson gave up his office and fled to Britain. There, he gave information about the colonies to the king. Hutchinson also wrote a book about the history of Massachusetts.

The Taxing Begins

Parliament passed the Sugar Act in 1764, taxing sugar, coffee, wine, and other goods in the colonies. After the Sugar Act, colonists protested an even bigger issue. James Otis Jr. raised the subject of taxation without representation. Through short booklets, newspaper articles, and Boston town meetings, Otis argued that British taxation was unfair because the colonies had no representatives in Parliament. Otis thought that Americans should

As royal governor of Massachusetts, Thomas Hutchinson tried to enforce the Stamp Act.

play a role in the governing of the colonies. "No taxation without representation" quickly became the cry expressing anti-British feelings.

The Stamp Act of 1765 followed the Sugar Act. The new act angered colonists because they were forced to pay tax on about 50 American-made paper items. Newspapers, legal documents, and playing cards all carried the tax stamp.

Shopkeepers refused to sell British goods. Instead, they offered for sale products brought in illegally from other countries. This action had a big, negative effect on the British economy.

Across America, colonists formed secret groups called the Sons of Liberty. They gathered at special places called liberty trees. American Patriots, who wanted independence from Britain, protested loudly against the Stamp Act. "Woe to British tax collectors and colonists who remain true to Britain," they said. Patriot mobs threatened these unfortunate people with tar and feathers. This punishment involved pouring hot tar over victims and rolling them in feathers. Scared stamp commissioners vanished from the colonies.

Britain Responds

On March 18, 1766, Britain canceled the Stamp Act. But Americans had no time to celebrate. On the same day, the Declaratory Act went into effect. This law said that Parliament had the right to make all laws for the American colonies.

The Townshend Acts became law in 1767. These acts taxed all glass, lead paint, paper, and tea arriving in America. Americans boycotted, or

Tarring and feathering, shown in this London drawing from 1774, was common in the American colonies.

refused to buy, British goods. British troops landed in Boston to enforce the acts, but British merchants still lost money. Many people demanded a stop to the taxes. In 1770, all taxes were removed, except the tea tax. Parliament kept it to prove that it still governed the colonies.

Groups of men called the Sons of Liberty met secretly to argue against the Stamp Act and other taxes.

Daughters of Liberty

The female version of the Sons of Liberty began around 1765. These Daughters of Liberty formed the first female political group in America. They peacefully boycotted taxed British goods. Women Patriots replaced foreign silks with cloth they spun themselves.

These women proudly wore country fashions. One Patriot from Massachusetts wrote that she would rather wrap herself in goatskin than buy goods "of a people who have insulted us in such a scandalous [dishonest] way." Women arranged Anti-Tea Leagues. Instead of sipping tea, they served pots of brewed herbs. Many people switched from drinking tea to drinking rye coffee.

Chapter Two

The American Cause Spreads

Bostonians were furious about the troops that had come to occupy their city during peacetime. Arguments grew between Patriots and British Redcoats, nicknamed for their bright red uniforms. The strain led to violence.

The Boston Massacre

On March 5, 1770, a fight broke out on Boston's King Street. A wig maker's assistant, Edward Garrick, made fun of a British officer. A British soldier whacked Garrick with his musket, which is a type of gun. Colonists soon formed a mob and threw iced snowballs at the soldier. The mob screamed insults, calling the Redcoat "lobster" and "bloody-back." The soldier ran to the Customs House, the center for British tax collectors. There, other British soldiers came to his aid.

During the Boston Massacre (above), blood was shed for the first time between British soldiers and American colonists.

Some people believe that on the dark, icy street, a soldier slipped after being struck. He accidentally fired his musket. In the confusion, shots thundered, and blood poured on the snow. Soldiers killed five colonists. News of the Boston Massacre spread throughout the colonies.

Samuel Adams

Born in Boston in 1722, Samuel Adams graduated from Harvard University and entered business. He failed as a beer maker, newspaper publisher, merchant, and tax collector. He often arrived late for meetings and had no head for figures. Although a poor businessman, Adams was an effective Patriot.

Adams started the first Committee of Correspondence in Boston in 1772. This group sent the latest Boston news in the form of letters up and down the Atlantic Coast. The idea caught on quickly in Massachussetts, and in a few months, there were more than 200 committees in that colony.

Other colonies followed Boston's lead. Various Committees of Correspondence compared notes on the American struggle with Britain. Later, the committees linked the colonies by spreading the dream of American independence.

Adams enjoyed stirring up trouble against Britain and its government. Outspoken, he gave passionate speeches on liberty. He wrote articles and pamphlets warning that the presence of British soldiers posed danger. These articles and thin booklets showed his strong feelings.

Adams's words could stir up a crowd. Wearing a rumpled suit and wrinkled stockings, Adams

Samuel Adams (left) was a second cousin to John Adams, who later became the second president of the United States.

addressed town meetings and led demonstrations. His voice rang out at gatherings in an old Boston meetinghouse called Faneuil Hall. This unlikely leader attracted other Patriots with his anti-British message.

Paul Revere

Silversmith and engraver Paul Revere became a friend of Adams. A silversmith makes or repairs silver objects. An engraver makes pictures that are printed from metal casts.

After the Boston Massacre, Revere engraved a copper plate showing Redcoats firing on unarmed Bostonians. While not a truthful version of the events, the engraving was printed across America. This political art had the desired effect. It made people angry with Britain.

Political Cartoons: Then and Now

Political cartoons are drawings that help explain an important event. The artist sometimes can sway people's opinions. These cartoons date far back in time. Benjamin Franklin is credited with drawing the first American political cartoon (below) in 1754.

At the time of the Boston Tea Party, artists created time-consuming engravings. Often, the news shown in the art was old before it reached an audience. This changed in 1884 when the *New York World* published a cartoon that made fun of a dinner honoring a politician. The dinner had been held only the night before. The timely cartoon led to the politician's loss of office, or defeat. Today, political cartoons are a popular feature of daily newspapers.

Chapter Three

Boston's Boiling Point

The tea tax caused colonists to worry about what the British government might tax next. If Parliament had control over tea, it might decide to control other goods. Colonial merchants could go out of business. Many Patriots refused to buy British tea and switched to tea smuggled illegally from other countries.

Yet, the tea tax cost American colonists only a few pennies each year. Even with a tax, this tea would be priced lower than smuggled tea. Parliament hoped the low price would tempt the colonists. But it did not, and tons of tea began to rot in British warehouses because of the American boycott.

The British East India Company

The British East India Company feared ruin. This powerful London firm shipped tea to other countries. Parliament offered the East India Company a monopoly. The company would have

Many Patriots stopped drinking British tea to protest the tea tax. Instead, like the people in the painting above, they sipped tea brought illegally into the colonies from other countries.

almost total control of all tea trade with the colonies. The deal between Parliament and the East India Company was called the Tea Act. It took effect in May 1773.

The East India Company sent agents across the Atlantic Ocean to sell the tea and collect taxes on any tea that was sold. Seven ships set sail for the American colonies in September 1773. They carried 500,000 pounds (226,800 kilograms) of tea. The ships' destinations were the ports of Boston, New York, Philadelphia, and Charleston, South Carolina.

Putting Fear in Tea Agents

Patriots, angry about the ships and their tea, threatened tea agents. Fearing harm, agents in every port except Boston canceled their orders or quit their jobs. Dockworkers refused to unload the tea in New York and Philadelphia. In Charleston, the tea was stored without being sold. Only the three ships heading for Boston Harbor sailed on for port.

Samuel Adams and the Boston Sons of Liberty gathered at the Liberty Tree in Hanover Square. Beneath the old elm, angry speakers demanded that the Boston tea agents give up their jobs.

British Tea

People in China first drank tea around 2700 B.C. Dutch traders introduced tea to Britain in 1657. Colonists drank about 1.2 million pounds (544,320 kilograms) of tea each year. It was Britain's fourth largest export to the colonies. An export is a product sold to another country.

The East India Company used a London export company, Davison Newman, to ship the teas that played a main role in the Boston Tea Party. The company is still in business today and sells a blend of tea named "Boston Harbour."

The Boston tea agents hid in a warehouse on Long Wharf and asked Hutchinson for help. The governor suggested that they move to Castle William, a British fort in Boston Harbor.

Hutchinson insisted that the tea ships land and made preparations for them to do so. He had two sons with ownership in the East India Company. They would make huge profits if the tea sold.

> BOSTON, December 2, 1773.
>
> WHEREAS it has been reported that a Permit will be given by the Custom-House for Landing the Tea now on Board a Veffel laying in this Harbour, commanded by Capt. HALL: THIS is to Remind the Publick, That it was folemnly voted by the Body of the People of this and the neighbouring Towns affembled at the Old-South Meeting-Houfe on Tuefday the 30th Day of November, that the faid Tea never fhould be landed in this Province, or pay one Farthing of Duty: And as the aiding or affifting in procuring or granting any fuch Permit for landing the faid Tea or any other Tea fo circumftanced, or in offering any Permit when obtained to the Mafter or Commander of the faid Ship, or any other Ship in the fame Situation, muft betray an inhuman Thirft for Blood, and will alfo in a great Meafure accelerate Confufion and Civil War: This is to affure fuch public Enemies of this Country, that they will be confidered and treated as Wretches unworthy to live, and will be made the firft Victims of our juft Refentment.
>
> The PEOPLE.
>
> N. B. Captain *Bruce* is arrived laden with the fame deteftable Commodity: and 'tis peremptorily demanded of him, and all concerned, that they comply with the fame Requifitions.
>
> A BOSTON WARNING.

Small, printed sheets of paper called handbills (right) spread through Boston. They warned people not to buy British tea.

The Liberty Tree

The Liberty Tree was a symbol of American independence. Patriots gathered there for meetings. During the Revolutionary War, British troops occupied Boston for a time. The soldiers cut down the Liberty Tree while stationed in the city in 1775.

"LIBERTY TREE."

The Tea Ships Dock

On November 28, the ship *Dartmouth* anchored at the Boston dock called Griffin's Wharf. The next morning, Adams sprang into action and held a meeting. Crowds of Patriots jammed Faneuil Hall. So many people attended the meeting that it had to be moved to a church called Old South Meeting House. The Patriots demanded that the tea return to Britain. The Committee of Correspondence and the Sons of Liberty sent armed Patriots to make sure that the tea was not unloaded for sale.

The second tea ship, the *Eleanor,* docked on December 1. The third ship, the *Beaver,* had been

Unlucky Tea

Abigail Adams, the wife of John Adams, wrote a letter from Boston describing the anchoring of the tea ships: "The tea, that baneful [unlucky] weed, is arrived . . . The flame is kindled [started], and like lightening it catches from soul to soul. I tremble when I think what may be the direful [horrible] consequences . . . and I dare not express half my fears." She could see that the tea's arrival would cause trouble.

delayed because people on board had smallpox, a disease that spreads easily and can cause death. After the *Beaver* arrived, Hutchinson set a deadline as part of a law made by Parliament.

Deciding about the Tea

According to Parliament's law, a ship full of tea could not simply go back to Britain without unloading its shipment. After 20 days, all tea taxes for a ship in a harbor had to be paid. If they were not, the British army would seize and unload the tea. Then the tea could be auctioned, or sold. Tea on the *Dartmouth* was due to be seized on December 17.

The royal governor commanded the British warships *Active* and *Kingfisher* to guard the harbor. Adams and the Committee of Correspondence made a decision. They would destroy the tea if it was not on its way back to Britain by midnight on December 16. Tension between Britain and the colonies was getting worse.

The *Beaver* was the third ship to arrive in Boston Harbor with tea. This photo shows a replica, or copy, of the *Beaver*.

Chapter Four

The Harbor Turns into a Teapot

Cold rain poured down on December 16. Bells in the steeple of the Old South Meeting House rang, inviting a crowd. Thousands of people filled the church, spilling out onto the streets. They awaited word from Francis Rotch, the 23-year-old son of the *Dartmouth*'s owner. Rotch had galloped off on horseback to the royal governor's country home. In a final effort, Rotch was requesting a pass to allow the *Dartmouth*'s return to Britain.

As they waited, colonists gave passionate speeches. Samuel Adams may have made statements such as: "If our trade be taxed, why not our lands, or produce, in short, everything we possess? They tax us without having legal representation. Fellow countrymen, we cannot afford to give a single inch! If we retreat now, everything we have done becomes useless! If Hutchinson will not send tea back to

At Old South Meeting House, the Patriots decided what would happen to the tea.

The Other Tea Parties

In the 1770s, the Boston Tea Party was known as the "Destruction of the Tea." It took about 50 years before the event was called the Boston Tea Party. The daring destruction inspired tea parties at other colonial ports. As the *London* tried to dock at New York on April 22, 1774, a mob rushed to destroy the tea that was aboard. Another ship met a similar fate at Greenwich, New Jersey, on December 22. Patriots at Annapolis, Maryland, set the *Peggy Stewart* afire on October 19. The entire tea cargo burned.

The original Boston Tea Party was so successful that the act was repeated. A second tea party took place in Boston on March 7, 1774. Again, colonists dumped tea into Boston Harbor. The value of the tea destroyed during both tea parties is estimated at $3 million in today's money. This loss was a huge expense to the British and the East India Company, whose storefront is shown here.

A Real Tea Chest

On November 20, 1902, John Hancock Foster made a special presentation. He gave the Boston Tea Party chapter of the Daughters of the American Revolution (DAR) an original tea chest. The wooden chest, which had been hand-painted in China, had been in Foster's family since the Boston Tea Party. The chest had stored tea on the journey from China to the American colonies. It has been on display at the DAR Museum in Washington, D.C., since 1969.

England [part of Britain], perhaps we can brew a pot of it especially for him!"

The Tension Mounts

Tempers were hot by the time Rotch returned from seeing Hutchinson. He had bad news. The British planned to seize the tea and unload it. People feared that this tea would soon be offered for sale at low prices that would be hard for people to resist. Adams thundered, "Gentlemen, this meeting can do nothing more to save the country!"

His words were greeted with war whoops. Dozens of men disguised as Mohawk Indians burst from the meetinghouse. Lawyers, blacksmiths, farmers, and merchants darkened their faces with chimney soot and red clay. They draped blankets over their clothing and clutched hatchets. The Patriots hoped these disguises would hide their identities from the British. What they were about to do was both dangerous and illegal.

For the Boston Tea Party, colonists disguised themselves as American Indians.

That Is a Lot of Tea!

The tea dumped during the Boston Tea Party was enough to make 26 million cups. That amount is almost enough to serve a cup to every man, woman, and child living in New York and Virginia today.

Headed for the Harbor

Shouts rang out as the church emptied. "Who knows how tea will mingle with salt water?" "Boston Harbor a teapot tonight!" The "Mohawks" marched toward Griffin's Wharf. A huge crowd followed them. Other Patriots joined, and the procession grew silent. At the harbor, about 50 men split into three groups. Each group boarded a tea ship.

Patriots ordered the ships' crews to help them open the holds, where the tea was stored beneath the decks. One by one, the heavy wooden chests of tea were hoisted on deck with ropes. Beneath the moon, the colonists chopped open the chests with their hatchets and dumped the tea into the harbor.

A Participant Speaks

"It was now evening, and I immediately dressed myself in the costume of an Indian, equipped with a small hatchet . . . [A]fter having painted my face and hands with coal dust in the shop of a blacksmith, I repaired [went] to Griffin's wharf, where the ships lay that contained the tea. When I first appeared in the street after being thus disguised, I fell in with many who were dressed, equipped and painted as I was, and who fell in with me and marched in order to the place of our destination . . . In about three hours from the time we went on board, we had thus broken and thrown overboard every tea chest to be found in the ship, while those in the other ships were disposing of the tea in the same way, at the same time. We were surrounded by British armed ships, but no attempt was made to resist us."

—George Hewes, participant in the Boston Tea Party

Boston Harbor was at low tide, and the tea piled into heaps. In three hours' time, 342 chests containing about 90,000 pounds (40,824 kilograms) of tea was ruined. The ships were undamaged except for one broken padlock that was replaced the next day.

The British sailors and soldiers who watched did not block the Patriots. There were no orders to stop the tea party. Unfortunately, some of the

This photo shows a modern-day reenactment of the Boston Tea Party.

party's own members betrayed it. Desperate for tea, a few men concealed tea leaves in pockets and boots. One man even hid tea in the lining of his coat. When the crowd waiting on shore discovered this cheating, they punished the tea thieves.

Cleaning Up

The task completed, the Patriots swept decks clean. They even emptied their shoes of stray tea leaves because they did not want to be caught. Not one speck of tea remained. As the men marched into the night, a fifer played music like

that of a flute. The next day, a song was created: "Rally Mohawks! bring out your axes, And tell King George we'll pay no taxes, on his foreign tea . . ."

British Admiral Montagu watched as the men went home. He called out, "Well boys, you have had a fine, pleasant evening for your Indian caper, haven't you? But mind, you have got to pay the fiddler yet!" He meant there would be a price to pay for their action.

The few Patriots who took tea during the Boston Tea Party were punished by other colonists.

Chapter Five

British Revenge

Paul Revere raced to spread the word in the colonies about the destruction of the tea. On horseback, he rode to New York and Philadelphia. He shared the account written by the Boston Committee of Correspondence. The Boston Tea Party brought hope of independence to the 13 colonies. Samuel Adams became a folk hero. His words at the Old South Meeting House had begun the Boston Tea Party.

It took one month before news of the destruction of the tea reached Britain. Once word reached him, King George III wanted Adams to be stopped. Furious, Parliament passed harsh laws in 1774 that Americans called the Intolerable Acts.

One of the acts called for Boston Harbor to be closed until Patriots paid for the ruined tea. For

ANNO DECIMO QUARTO

Georgii III. Regis.

CAP. XIX.

An Act to discontinue, in such Manner, and for
such Time as are therein mentioned, the
landing and discharging, lading or shipping,
of Goods, Wares, and Merchandise, at the
Town, and within the Harbour, of *Boston*, in
the Province of *Massachuset's Bay*, in *North
America.*

FIRST PAGE OF THE BOSTON
PORT BILL
Reduced facsimile

King George III (above)
issued an order (left) to
punish Bostonians for
the Boston Tea Party.

Did You Know?

After the Revolutionary War, Samuel Adams served as governor of Massachusetts from 1794 to 1797.

Bostonians who relied on the sea for their living, this law meant ruin. Every colony came to Boston's aid. They sent flour, sheep, and money.

War and Independence

That September, leaders from all colonies except Georgia formed the First Continental Congress. These men gathered in Philadelphia to talk about solving their problems with Britain. Then, in April 1775, colonists fought British soldiers in the Battles of Lexington and Concord. The Revolutionary War

(1775–1783) had begun. Battles continued for years until the British surrendered at Yorktown, Virginia, in October 1781. Britain finally recognized America's independence with the signing of the Treaty of Paris in 1783.

Boston, often called the "cradle of liberty," had helped give birth to a new country—the United States of America. The struggle and success of the Patriots continues to inspire countries around the world.

British troops surrendered to the Americans at the Battle of Yorktown, the last major fight of the Revolutionary War.

TIMELINE

The French and
Indian War ends.

The Stamp Act is removed; the
Declaratory Act takes effect.

Parliament passes
the Sugar Act.

The Townshend
Acts are passed.

1763   1764   1765   1766   1767   1768

Parliament passes the Stamp
Act; American colonists form
Sons of Liberty and destroy the
Boston home of Royal Governor
Thomas Hutchinson.

British troops land
in Boston to enforce
the Townshend Acts.

British surrender at Yorktown, ending the Revolutionary War.

Battles of Lexington and Concord start the Revolutionary War.

| 1770 | 1772 | 1773 | 1774 | 1775 | 1781 |

The Tea Act takes effect; the Boston Tea Party takes place.

Boston Massacre

First Committee of Correspondence formed

Parliament passes the Intolerable Acts; the First Continental Congress meets.

Glossary

boycott (BOI-kot)—to refuse to buy certain goods as a means of protest

Customs House (KUHSS-tuhmz HOUSS)—the building where the British collected taxes and cleared ships to enter ports

export (EK-sport)—a product sold to another country

hold (HOHLD)—the cargo area below a ship's deck

intolerable (in-TOL-ur-uh-buhl)—unbearable

liberty tree (LIB-ur-tee TREE)—a tree where colonists met to discuss public events and to protest British laws

monopoly (muh-NOP-uh-lee)—a service or the supply of a product completely controlled by one party

Parliament (PAR-luh-muhnt)—Britain's governing body of lawmakers

Patriot (PAY-tree-uht)—an American colonist who disagreed with British rule of the colonies

smallpox (SMAWL-poks)—a disease that spreads easily from person to person, causing chills, fever, and pimples that scar; smallpox often causes death.

taxation (taks-AY-shuhn)—a requirement that people and businesses pay money to support a government

For Further Reading

Burgan, Michael. *The Boston Tea Party.* We the People. Minneapolis: Compass Point Books, 2001.

Edwards, Pam. *Boston Tea Party.* New York: Putnam, 2001.

Kroll, Steven. *The Boston Tea Party.* New York: Holiday House, 1998.

Moore, Kay. *If You Lived at the Time of the American Revolution.* New York: Scholastic, 1997.

O'Neill, Laurie A. *The Boston Tea Party.* Spotlight on American History. Brookfield, Conn.: Millbrook Press, 1996.

Todd, Anne. *The Revolutionary War.* America Goes to War. Mankato, Minn.: Capstone Books, 2001.

Places of Interest

Boston Tea Party Ship and Museum
Congress Street Bridge
Boston, MA 02210
A step back in history; the *Beaver II* was made to look like the original *Beaver* boarded during the Boston Tea Party. On the ship, people reenact the Boston Tea Party. The museum offers films and exhibits that bring the uprising to life.

Faneuil Hall
75 State Street
Boston, MA 02109
Where protests against British policy took place; today visitors can listen in on historical talks.

Old Granary Burying Ground
Near the corner of Park and Tremont Streets
Boston, Massachusetts
This cemetery contains gravestones dating back to the 1660s and includes the final resting spots for Patriots Samuel Adams, John Hancock, and Paul Revere, along with the victims of the Boston Massacre.

Old South Meeting House
310 Washington Street
Boston, Massachusetts
http://www.oldsouthmeetinghouse.org
Where the Boston Tea Party had its roots; today, this house of worship invites visitors to listen to a tape reenacting speeches encouraging the tea party.

Internet Sites

The Boston Tea Party
http://www.pbs.org/ktca/liberty/chronicle/bostonteaparty-edenton.html
Contains information on the Boston Tea Party

The Boston Tea Party Chapter of Daughters of the American Revolution
http://members.aol.com/massdar/Massachusetts_DAR/teaparty.htm
Includes a list of participants in the Boston Tea Party and other Internet sites to visit

Boston Tea Party Ship and Museum
http://www.bostonteapartyship.com
Has online activities such as building the *Beaver* and reading *The Tea Party Gazette*

The History Place: American Revolution
http://www.historyplace.com/unitedstates/revolution/teaparty.htm
Provides a full account of the Boston Tea Party by participant George Hewes

KidInfo: American Revolution
http://www.kidinfo.com/American_History/American_Revolution.html
Offers many links related to the American Revolution and its various events

Index